BIRD-EATING SPIDERS

THE SPIDER DISCOVERY LIBRARY

Louise Martin

Rourke Enterprises, Inc.
Vero Beach, Florida 32964

LIBRARY OF CONGRESS
Library of Congress Cataloging-in-Publication Data

Martin, Louise, 1955-
  Bird eating spiders/by Louise Martin.

    p. cm. — (The Spider discovery library)
  Includes index.
  Summary: Describes the physical characteristics, habits,
and natural environment of some of the world's largest
spiders that often build their nests in trees and feed on
birds and small animals.
  ISBN 0-86592-966-1
  1. Tarantulas — Juvenile literature. [1. Tarantulas.2.
Spiders.] I. Title. II. Series: Martin, Louise, 1955-
Spider discovery library.
QL458.42.T5M36   1988   88-5976
595.4'4 - dc19   CIP
                                           AC

*Title page photo: Bird-eating spiders
like this often live in trees*

TABLE OF CONTENTS

BIRD-EATING SPIDERS

Bird-eating spiders, like the hairy North American tarantulas, are members of the *Theraphosidae* family of spiders. They are sometimes called tree spiders, because they often build their nests in trees. The spiders are commonly called bird-eating spiders, since they are known to eat birds as part of their diet.

An East African bird-eating spider

HOW THEY LOOK

Bird-eating spiders are some of the biggest spiders in the world. The largest bird-eating spiders live in South America. Some South American **species** can have bodies three inches across. Including their thick, strong legs, these spiders can span nearly ten inches. Bird-eating spiders have very hairy bodies and legs. Their poison fangs are hard and shiny.

A huge bird-eating spider from Peru, South America

WHERE THEY LIVE

Bird-eating spiders are found in many parts of the world. They are **tropical** spiders, living in warm climates. Bird-eating spiders are common in the southern United States, South America, tropical Africa, India and the Far East, and parts of Australia. The Asian species of bird-eating spiders are not as huge and fearsome as those found in northern South America.

A hairy Haitian bird-eating spider

THEIR HOMES

Some bird-eating spiders build nests in rock **crevices** or under the loose bark of a tree. These nest-building spiders do not spin webs. They remain in their nests during the day and come out at night to hunt for food. One species of bird-eating spider in South America is known to live in a burrow, like some of the other *Mygalomorph* spiders.

Bird-eating spiders sometimes build nests in rock crevices

Bird-eating spiders' webs are very thick

A baby spider hatches from its egg

THEIR WEBS

Other species of bird-eating spiders spin webs instead of building nests. The webs are often found in the roofs of houses and across the corners of rooms. Bird-eating spiders' webs are very thick and closely woven. They are important for the capture of the spiders' **prey**. Once the prey has become entangled in the web, it is almost impossible for it to escape.

Bird-eating spiders' hairy legs can make you itch

BABY BIRD-EATING SPIDERS

Some of the larger *Mygalomorph* spiders, like bird-eating spiders, can lay up to three thousand eggs in one batch. The bird-eating spiders' eggs are quite big. Each egg may be as large as a small pea. The female bird-eating spiders wrap the eggs in a silk **cocoon** and wait for them to hatch. When the **spiderlings** hatch from the eggs they are already bigger than some fully grown spiders.

A bird-eating spider eats a bird

BIRD-EATING SPIDERS AND PEOPLE

All spiders inject **venom** into their prey before they
feed. Not all spiders' venom is harmful to man.
Bird-eating spiders' bites are painful, but they are not
dangerous. Bird-eating spiders can be handled
without being bitten, but the hairs on their bodies and
legs can make you itchy. Most spiders are quite shy
and only bite if they are frightened.

*A bird-eating spider at the entrance
to its burrow*

WHAT THEY EAT

Bird-eating spiders also prey on animals that live on the ground. Many feed on mice and lizards. Bird-eating spiders have been known to attack hens that are waiting for their chicks to hatch. Once the venom has been injected into the body of the prey, it is only a matter of time before it dies.

A bird-eating spider carrying its egg sac

PREY

In spite of their name, bird-eating spiders live mostly on ants and other insects. Because of their size, they can easily attack and eat birds and small animals. Small birds often become trapped in the spiders' thick webs which they spin between the branches of trees. The bird-eating spiders **paralyze** the birds with their venom, and feed on them.

Glossary

cocoon (co COON) — a silk wrap used to protects eggs

crevices (CRE vic es) — cracks

paralyze (PAR a lyze) — to make a person or animal unable to move

prey (PREY) — an animal that is hunted for food

species (SPE cies) — a scientific term meaning type or kind

spiderlings (SPI der lings) — baby spiders

tropical (TRO pi cal) — hot

venom (VEN om) — poison

INDEX